CHECKERBOARD BIOGRAPHY LIBRARY

U.S. PRESIDENTS

The
United States Presidents

JAMES MADISON

ABDO Publishing Company

Megan M. Gunderson

visit us at
www.abdopublishing.com

Published by ABDO Publishing Company, 8000 West 78th Street, Edina, Minnesota 55439.
Copyright © 2009 by Abdo Consulting Group, Inc. International copyrights reserved in all
countries. No part of this book may be reproduced in any form without written permission from the
publisher. The Checkerboard Library™ is a trademark and logo of ABDO Publishing Company.

Printed in the United States of America, North Mankato, Minnesota.
012009 032013

Cover Photo: Getty Images
Interior Photos: Alamy pp. 11, 13; AP Images pp. 9, 14, 21; Corbis pp. 5, 22, 24;
    Getty Images pp. 16, 25, 29; iStockphoto p. 32; Library of Congress p. 12;
    National Archives pp. 15, 17, 19, 20, 26; North Wind p. 27; Picture History p. 24

Editor: Heidi M.D. Elston
Art Direction & Cover Design: Neil Klinepier
Interior Design: Neil Klinepier

Library of Congress Cataloging-in-Publication Data

Gunderson, Megan M., 1981-
 James Madison / Megan M. Gunderson.
    p. cm. -- (The United States presidents)
 Includes index.
 ISBN 978-1-60453-465-8
 1. Madison, James, 1751-1836--Juvenile literature. 2. Presidents--United States--Biography--
Juvenile literature. I. Title.

 E342.G86 2009
 973.5'1092--dc22
 [B]
                            2008044331

CONTENTS

JAMES MADISON

James Madison was the fourth president of the United States. He grew up in Virginia and went to college in New Jersey. After he graduated, Madison was elected to his first public office.

Soon, the **American Revolution** began. As the war for independence raged on, Madison became an important political leader. He served in the Continental Congress and the Virginia legislature.

Madison also attended the **Constitutional** Convention. There, he helped plan how to run the new government. He used what he knew about political history to help write the U.S. Constitution. For this reason, Madison is known as the Father of the Constitution.

Madison was then elected to the U.S. House of Representatives. As a congressman, he sponsored the Bill of Rights. Under President Thomas Jefferson, Madison served as **secretary of state**. In this role, he helped with the Louisiana Purchase.

When Jefferson left office in 1809, Madison became president. President Madison led the nation through the War of 1812.

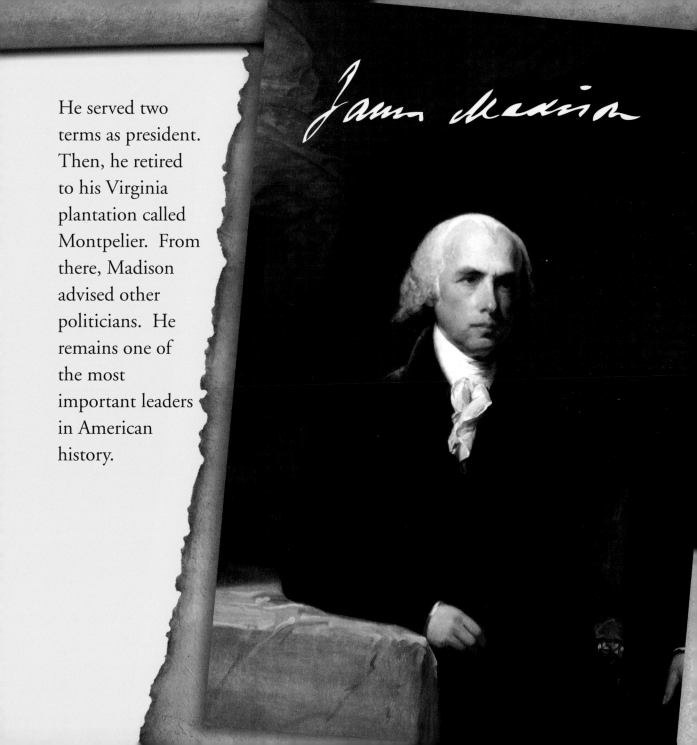

He served two terms as president. Then, he retired to his Virginia plantation called Montpelier. From there, Madison advised other politicians. He remains one of the most important leaders in American history.

TIMELINE

1751 - On March 16, James Madison was born in Port Conway, Virginia.

1771 - Madison graduated from the College of New Jersey in Princeton.

1774 - Madison was elected to the Orange County Committee of Safety.

1776 - At the Virginia Convention in May, Madison helped write Virginia's new constitution; Madison began serving in the Virginia legislature.

1778 - Madison began serving in the Virginia Council of State.

1780 - In March, Madison began serving in the Continental Congress.

1787 - Madison attended the Constitutional Convention, where he helped plan the U.S. Constitution; on September 17, Madison and 38 other delegates signed the U.S. Constitution.

1789 - Madison began serving in the U.S. House of Representatives, where he sponsored the Bill of Rights.

1794 - On September 15, Madison married Dolley Payne Todd.

1801 - President Thomas Jefferson appointed Madison secretary of state.

1803 - Madison supported the Louisiana Purchase.

1809 - On March 4, Madison became the fourth U.S. president.

1812 - The War of 1812 began on June 18; Madison was reelected president.

1814 - On December 24, the United States and Great Britain signed the Treaty of Ghent.

1836 - On June 28, James Madison died.

DID YOU KNOW?

James Madison was the smallest U.S. president. He was just five feet six inches (1.7 m) tall. And, he only weighed about 100 pounds (45 kg)! In a letter, Dolley Payne Todd called her future husband "the great little Madison."

While Madison was president, two new states were admitted. Louisiana joined the United States in 1812. Indiana followed in 1816.

During the War of 1812, Francis Scott Key wrote "The Star-Spangled Banner." In 1931, this officially became the national anthem.

On April 20, 1812, George Clinton became the first vice president to die in office.

In 1752, Great Britain adopted a new calendar. This changed Madison's birthday from March 5 to March 16.

COLONIAL VIRGINIA

James Madison was born on March 16, 1751, in Port Conway, Virginia. At the time, Virginia was a British colony.

The Madison family was large. James was the oldest of 12 children. His father was also named James Madison. He ran the family plantation, Montpelier. About 100 slaves worked on this large plantation.

James's mother was Eleanor "Nelly" Conway. She began his education at home by teaching him to read and write. James soon fell in love with reading.

When James was 11, he went away to school. He attended Donald Robertson's boarding school in King and Queen County, Virginia. James studied science, mathematics, history, and literature. He also studied languages such as Latin, Greek, French, and Italian.

FAST FACTS

BORN - March 16, 1751

WIFE - Dolley Payne Todd
(1768–1849)

CHILDREN - None

POLITICAL PARTY - Democratic-Republican

AGE AT INAUGURATION - 57

YEARS SERVED - 1809–1817

VICE PRESIDENTS - George Clinton, Elbridge Gerry

DIED - June 28, 1836, age 85

8

Montpelier remained James's home for his entire life.

    At 16, James returned home to Montpelier. He began studying with a **tutor** named Thomas Martin. Martin was a minister in Orange County, Virginia. After two years of studying, James was ready for college.

COLLEGE OF NEW JERSEY

Martin encouraged James to attend the College of New Jersey in Princeton. So in 1769, James moved to New Jersey. He rode a horse all the way there!

James studied **debate**, Greek, Latin, science, and literature at school. He and his classmates also discussed current events. At the time, many colonists were upset by British rule. They felt laws such as the **Stamp Act** had taxed the colonists unfairly. James agreed. So, he joined the American Whig Society. This was an anti-British student club.

College usually took four years to complete. But James finished in just two! He graduated in 1771. James then stayed in Princeton for an extra six months. During that time, he studied Hebrew and philosophy. Then in 1772, James returned to Montpelier. He studied law, history, and politics at home.

The College of New Jersey was founded in 1746. In 1896, it was renamed Princeton University.

VIRGINIA LEADER

In 1774, Madison was elected to his first public office. He earned a position on the Orange County Committee of Safety. Madison's father was the chairman of this group. It was in charge of the local **militia**. And, it provided local government.

The following year, the **American Revolution** began. Madison joined the Orange County militia as a colonel. Yet his health was poor. So, he did not serve long.

In May 1776, Madison became a delegate to the Virginia Convention in Williamsburg. The convention called for Virginia's independence from Great Britain.

Madison helped write Virginia's new **constitution**. The convention adopted it on June 29. It became the model for the U.S. Constitution and other state constitutions.

Today, visitors to Colonial Williamsburg can experience life as it was in Madison's time.

Meanwhile, other colonies were calling for independence from Great Britain. On July 4, 1776, the Continental Congress approved the Declaration of Independence. This essay declared all the colonies "Free and Independent States."

Madison also served in the Virginia legislature in 1776. There, he met Thomas Jefferson. The two would work closely together for the rest of their careers.

Jefferson became a lifelong friend to Madison.

Madison and Jefferson wanted to improve Virginia's laws on religion and education. They fought to guarantee freedom of religion. The two also sought free public education for all Virginians. And, they asked the state to support college education.

Next, Madison was elected to the Virginia Council of State. This group advised the governor of Virginia. Madison served in it from 1778 to 1779. First, Madison served under Governor Patrick Henry. Then, he served under Jefferson when he became governor.

In CONGRESS. July 4, 1776.

The unanimous Declaration of the thirteen united States of America.

The Declaration of Independence

CONTINENTAL CONGRESS

In March 1780, Madison began serving in the Continental Congress. Delegates from each state made up this group. It served as a temporary government for all the states.

By 1781, all the states had approved the **Articles of Confederation**. Under the articles, Congress had the power to declare war and raise an army. However, it could not collect taxes. This made it difficult to pay national **debts**.

So, Madison worked to increase the government's power to raise **revenue**. He also requested more money to support the army during the **American Revolution**.

At 29, Madison was the youngest member of the Continental Congress.

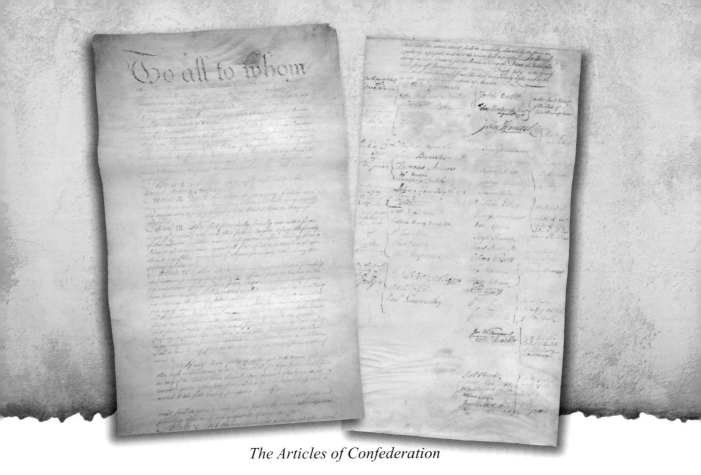

The Articles of Confederation

Madison also worked to establish the Mississippi River as the nation's western boundary. This would allow for increased trade. His plan was achieved in 1783 under the Treaty of Paris. This treaty also ended the **American Revolution**.

The same year, Madison retired from Congress. In 1784, he returned to the Virginia legislature. There, Madison continued fighting for freedom of religion.

U.S. Constitution

By 1786, Massachusetts farmers were upset about high taxes and falling farm prices. Mobs formed to stop local courts from conducting business. And, Daniel Shays and others carried out additional attacks.

Under the **Articles of Confederation**, the national government could not help Massachusetts end the fighting. Shays's **Rebellion** highlighted the need for a stronger central government.

The same year, Madison attended the Annapolis Convention in Maryland. There, delegates agreed that the Articles of Confederation needed to be revised. For this purpose, they planned the **Constitutional** Convention.

Madison attended the convention in 1787. There, Governor Edmund Randolph presented Madison's Virginia Plan. The proposal provided for a stronger national government. However, the power would be divided between three branches. These are the executive, judicial, and legislative branches.

The separation of powers would keep the government from being too strong. This became the basic principle of the U.S. **Constitution**.

On September 17, Madison and 38 delegates signed the U.S. Constitution. Madison, Alexander Hamilton, and John Jay then wrote a series of 85 essays. Together, they are called the Federalist papers. These essays explained and promoted the U.S. Constitution.

The U.S. Constitution

NEW GOVERNMENT

In 1789, George Washington became the first U.S. president. Madison helped write his **inaugural** speech. He also helped Washington choose the first **cabinet** members.

The same year, Madison began serving in the U.S. House of Representatives. This group was part of the new legislative branch described in the U.S. **Constitution**.

In the House, Madison sponsored the Bill of Rights. These are the first ten **amendments** to the U.S. Constitution. They provide certain rights, such as freedom of speech and freedom of religion. Madison served in the House until 1797.

The Bill of Rights

Meanwhile, Madison had met a widow named Dolley Payne Todd. From her first marriage, she had a son named John Payne Todd. Madison and Dolley married on September 15, 1794. They had no children of their own. But together, they raised Dolley's son.

In 1798, President John Adams passed the Sedition Act. This law made it a crime to speak out against the government.

Madison believed the law limited freedom of speech. So,

Before becoming First Lady, Dolley Madison acted as White House hostess under widowed president Thomas Jefferson.

he fought against it by writing the Virginia Resolutions. With these, he argued that the new law was **unconstitutional**. The following year, Madison returned to the Virginia legislature.

SECRETARY OF STATE

President Adams was supported by the **Federalist** Party. Madison and Jefferson had formed the **Democratic-Republican** Party to oppose it. The two parties disagreed about the powers of the national government. With Madison's support, Jefferson defeated Adams in the 1800 presidential election.

Madison was the second secretary of state to later become president.

22

In 1801, Jefferson became the third U.S. president. That year, he asked Madison to be **secretary of state**. Secretary Madison felt the port of New Orleans was important to U.S. trade. So, he thought the United States should purchase this land from France.

In 1803, Madison supported the Louisiana Purchase. With this, the United States gained the land between the Mississippi River and the Rocky Mountains. The area included New Orleans. And, it doubled the size of the nation.

Meanwhile, Great Britain and France were at war. The United States tried to remain **neutral**. However, both nations were attacking U.S. ships and capturing American sailors.

In 1807, Madison supported Jefferson's Embargo Act. This law closed U.S. ports to all foreign trade. However, the act caused problems for U.S. businesses. So two years later, Jefferson replaced it with the Non-Intercourse Act. Madison supported this new law. It only banned trade with Britain and France.

PRESIDENT MADISON

In 1808, Madison ran for president. His **Federalist** opponent was Charles C. Pinckney of South Carolina. Madison won 122 electoral votes to Pinckney's 47. George Clinton was elected Madison's vice president.

On March 4, 1809, Madison was **inaugurated** the fourth U.S. president. Immediately, he faced many challenges.

France and Great Britain remained at war. Madison still tried to keep the United States **neutral**. But at sea, British attacks on U.S. ships continued.

President Madison felt he had no choice but to go to war. He asked Congress to declare war on Great Britain. On June 18, 1812, the War of 1812 began.

That year, Madison faced reelection. He defeated Federalist DeWitt Clinton of New York. Elbridge Gerry of Massachusetts was elected Madison's new vice president.

George Clinton

Elbridge Gerry

PRESIDENT MADISON'S CABINET

FIRST TERM
MARCH 4, 1809–MARCH 4, 1813

- **STATE** – Robert Smith
  James Monroe (from 1811)
- **TREASURY** – Albert Gallatin
- **WAR** – John Smith
  William Eustis (from April 8, 1809)
  John Armstrong (from February 5, 1813)
- **NAVY** – Robert Smith
  Paul Hamilton (from May 15, 1809)
  William Jones (from January 19, 1813)
- **ATTORNEY GENERAL** – Caesar A. Rodney
  William Pinkney (from January 6, 1812)

SECOND TERM
MARCH 4, 1813–MARCH 4, 1817

- **STATE** – James Monroe
- **TREASURY** – Albert Gallatin
  George W. Campbell (from February 9, 1814)
  Alexander J. Dallas (from October 14, 1814)
  William H. Crawford (from October 22, 1816)
- **WAR** – John Armstrong
  James Monroe (from October 1, 1814)
  William H. Crawford (from August 8, 1815)
- **NAVY** – William Jones
  Benjamin W. Crowninshield (from January 16, 1815)
- **ATTORNEY GENERAL** – William Pinkney
  Richard Rush (from February 11, 1814)

Madison was **inaugurated** on March 4, 1813. During his second term, the War of 1812 remained challenging. In the beginning, Congress refused to help build up the military. And, many generals were older men who had fought during the **American Revolution**. So, the army suffered many defeats on land.

Yet the navy was successful at sea. And by 1814, the average age of generals had fallen from 60 to 36. As a result, the United States began winning more battles.

Still, British soldiers attacked Washington, D.C., on August 24, 1814. They burned down the White House and other government buildings. Finally on December 24, the United States and Great Britain signed the Treaty of Ghent.

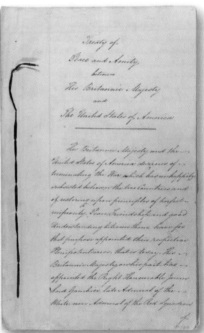

The Treaty of Ghent

SUPREME
COURT
APPOINTMENTS

GABRIEL DUVALL - 1811
JOSEPH STORY - 1812

With this, the two nations agreed to end the War of 1812.

Mrs. Madison escaped with George Washington's portrait before the White House burned.

During the same month, **Federalists** began the Hartford Convention in Connecticut. There, delegates from five New England states met. They expressed their opposition to the War of 1812. The delegates felt the federal government had left New England unprotected during the war. So, they wanted more independence for their states.

Many people feared the New England states planned to leave the United States. So, the Federalists and their ideas were seen as unpatriotic. As a result, President Madison became even more popular. In addition, the Federalist Party soon died out.

BACK TO MONTPELIER

Madison's **secretary of state**, James Monroe, was elected president in 1816. The next year, the Madisons retired to Montpelier. Still, Madison remained politically active. He gave Monroe advice about foreign relations. And, people visited Madison's home to discuss politics.

In Virginia, Madison worked on his plantation. He tried many new farming methods. Madison also maintained his friendship with Jefferson. Jefferson established the University of Virginia in Charlottesville in 1819. Madison served on the university's Board of Visitors. Then after Jefferson's death in 1826, he became **rector**.

In 1829, Madison attended the Virginia **constitutional** convention. There, he tried to revise laws related to voting rights and slavery. This was his last public office. On June 28, 1836, James Madison died.

Today, Madison is remembered as the Father of the **Constitution**. He also helped expand the nation's borders while serving as **secretary of state**. Then as president, he successfully led the nation through the War of 1812. James Madison is one of the most important early leaders in U.S. history.

In retirement, Madison worked to end the practice of slavery.

OFFICE OF THE PRESIDENT

BRANCHES OF GOVERNMENT

The U.S. government is divided into three branches. They are the executive, legislative, and judicial branches. This division is called a separation of powers. Each branch has some power over the others. This is called a system of checks and balances.

EXECUTIVE BRANCH

The executive branch enforces laws. It is made up of the president, the vice president, and the president's cabinet. The president represents the United States around the world. He or she oversees relations with other countries and signs treaties. The president signs bills into law and appoints officials and federal judges. He or she also leads the military and manages government workers.

LEGISLATIVE BRANCH

The legislative branch makes laws, maintains the military, and regulates trade. It also has the power to declare war. This branch consists of the Senate and the House of Representatives. Together, these two houses make up Congress. Each state has two senators. A state's population determines the number of representatives it has.

JUDICIAL BRANCH

The judicial branch interprets laws. It consists of district courts, courts of appeals, and the Supreme Court. District courts try cases. If a person disagrees with a trial's outcome, he or she may appeal. If the courts of appeals support the ruling, a person may appeal to the Supreme Court. The Supreme Court also makes sure that laws follow the U.S. Constitution.

QUALIFICATIONS FOR OFFICE

To be president, a person must meet three requirements. A candidate must be at least 35 years old and a natural-born U.S. citizen. He or she must also have lived in the United States for at least 14 years.

ELECTORAL COLLEGE

The U.S. presidential election is an indirect election. Voters from each state choose electors to represent them in the Electoral College. The number of electors from each state is based on population. Each elector has one electoral vote. Electors are pledged to cast their vote for the candidate who receives the highest number of popular votes in their state. A candidate must receive the majority of Electoral College votes to win.

TERM OF OFFICE

Each president may be elected to two four-year terms. Sometimes, a president may only be elected once. This happens if he or she served more than two years of the previous president's term.

The presidential election is held on the Tuesday after the first Monday in November. The president is sworn in on January 20 of the following year. At that time, he or she takes the oath of office:

I do solemnly swear (or affirm) that I will faithfully execute the office of President of the United States, and will to the best of my ability, preserve, protect and defend the Constitution of the United States.

LINE OF SUCCESSION

The Presidential Succession Act of 1947 defines who becomes president if the president cannot serve. The vice president is first in the line of succession. Next are the Speaker of the House and the President Pro Tempore of the Senate. If none of these individuals is able to serve, the office falls to the president's cabinet members. They would take office in the order in which each department was created:

Secretary of State

Secretary of the Treasury

Secretary of Defense

Attorney General

Secretary of the Interior

Secretary of Agriculture

Secretary of Commerce

Secretary of Labor

Secretary of Health and Human Services

Secretary of Housing and Urban Development

Secretary of Transportation

Secretary of Energy

Secretary of Education

Secretary of Veterans Affairs

Secretary of Homeland Security

BENEFITS

- While in office, the president receives a salary of $400,000 each year. He or she lives in the White House and has 24-hour Secret Service protection.

- The president may travel on a Boeing 747 jet called Air Force One. The airplane can accommodate 70 passengers. It has kitchens, a dining room, sleeping areas, and a conference room. It also has fully equipped offices with the latest communications systems. Air Force One can fly halfway around the world before needing to refuel. It can even refuel in flight!

- If the president wishes to travel by car, he or she uses Cadillac One. Cadillac One is a Cadillac Deville. It has been modified with heavy armor and communications systems. The president takes Cadillac One along when visiting other countries if secure transportation will be needed.

- The president also travels on a helicopter called Marine One. Like the presidential car, Marine One accompanies the president when traveling abroad if necessary.

- Sometimes, the president needs to get away and relax with family and friends. Camp David is the official presidential retreat. It is located in the cool, wooded mountains in Maryland. The U.S. Navy maintains the retreat, and the U.S. Marine Corps keeps it secure. The camp offers swimming, tennis, golf, and hiking.

- When the president leaves office, he or she receives Secret Service protection for ten more years. He or she also receives a yearly pension of $191,300 and funding for office space, supplies, and staff.

PRESIDENTS AND THEIR TERMS

PRESIDENT	PARTY	TOOK OFFICE	LEFT OFFICE	TERMS SERVED	VICE PRESIDENT
George Washington	None	April 30, 1789	March 4, 1797	Two	John Adams
John Adams	Federalist	March 4, 1797	March 4, 1801	One	Thomas Jefferson
Thomas Jefferson	Democratic-Republican	March 4, 1801	March 4, 1809	Two	Aaron Burr, George Clinton
James Madison	Democratic-Republican	March 4, 1809	March 4, 1817	Two	George Clinton, Elbridge Gerry
James Monroe	Democratic-Republican	March 4, 1817	March 4, 1825	Two	Daniel D. Tompkins
John Quincy Adams	Democratic-Republican	March 4, 1825	March 4, 1829	One	John C. Calhoun
Andrew Jackson	Democrat	March 4, 1829	March 4, 1837	Two	John C. Calhoun, Martin Van Buren
Martin Van Buren	Democrat	March 4, 1837	March 4, 1841	One	Richard M. Johnson
William H. Harrison	Whig	March 4, 1841	April 4, 1841	Died During First Term	John Tyler
John Tyler	Whig	April 6, 1841	March 4, 1845	Completed Harrison's Term	Office Vacant
James K. Polk	Democrat	March 4, 1845	March 4, 1849	One	George M. Dallas
Zachary Taylor	Whig	March 5, 1849	July 9, 1850	Died During First Term	Millard Fillmore

PRESIDENT	PARTY	TOOK OFFICE	LEFT OFFICE	TERMS SERVED	VICE PRESIDENT
Millard Fillmore	Whig	July 10, 1850	March 4, 1853	Completed Taylor's Term	Office Vacant
Franklin Pierce	Democrat	March 4, 1853	March 4, 1857	One	William R.D. King
James Buchanan	Democrat	March 4, 1857	March 4, 1861	One	John C. Breckinridge
Abraham Lincoln	Republican	March 4, 1861	April 15, 1865	Served One Term, Died During Second Term	Hannibal Hamlin, Andrew Johnson
Andrew Johnson	Democrat	April 15, 1865	March 4, 1869	Completed Lincoln's Second Term	Office Vacant
Ulysses S. Grant	Republican	March 4, 1869	March 4, 1877	Two	Schuyler Colfax, Henry Wilson
Rutherford B. Hayes	Republican	March 3, 1877	March 4, 1881	One	William A. Wheeler
James A. Garfield	Republican	March 4, 1881	September 19, 1881	Died During First Term	Chester Arthur
Chester Arthur	Republican	September 20, 1881	March 4, 1885	Completed Garfield's Term	Office Vacant
Grover Cleveland	Democrat	March 4, 1885	March 4, 1889	One	Thomas A. Hendricks
Benjamin Harrison	Republican	March 4, 1889	March 4, 1893	One	Levi P. Morton
Grover Cleveland	Democrat	March 4, 1893	March 4, 1897	One	Adlai E. Stevenson
William McKinley	Republican	March 4, 1897	September 14, 1901	Served One Term, Died During Second Term	Garret A. Hobart, Theodore Roosevelt

PRESIDENT	PARTY	TOOK OFFICE	LEFT OFFICE	TERMS SERVED	VICE PRESIDENT
Theodore Roosevelt	Republican	September 14, 1901	March 4, 1909	Completed McKinley's Second Term, Served One Term	Office Vacant, Charles Fairbanks
William Taft	Republican	March 4, 1909	March 4, 1913	One	James S. Sherman
Woodrow Wilson	Democrat	March 4, 1913	March 4, 1921	Two	Thomas R. Marshall
Warren G. Harding	Republican	March 4, 1921	August 2, 1923	Died During First Term	Calvin Coolidge
Calvin Coolidge	Republican	August 3, 1923	March 4, 1929	Completed Harding's Term, Served One Term	Office Vacant, Charles Dawes
Herbert Hoover	Republican	March 4, 1929	March 4, 1933	One	Charles Curtis
Franklin D. Roosevelt	Democrat	March 4, 1933	April 12, 1945	Served Three Terms, Died During Fourth Term	John Nance Garner, Henry A. Wallace, Harry S. Truman
Harry S. Truman	Democrat	April 12, 1945	January 20, 1953	Completed Roosevelt's Fourth Term, Served One Term	Office Vacant, Alben Barkley
Dwight D. Eisenhower	Republican	January 20, 1953	January 20, 1961	Two	Richard Nixon
John F. Kennedy	Democrat	January 20, 1961	November 22, 1963	Died During First Term	Lyndon B. Johnson
Lyndon B. Johnson	Democrat	November 22, 1963	January 20, 1969	Completed Kennedy's Term, Served One Term	Office Vacant, Hubert H. Humphrey
Richard Nixon	Republican	January 20, 1969	August 9, 1974	Completed First Term, Resigned During Second Term	Spiro T. Agnew, Gerald Ford

PRESIDENTS 26–37, 1901–1974

PRESIDENT	PARTY	TOOK OFFICE	LEFT OFFICE	TERMS SERVED	VICE PRESIDENT
Gerald Ford	Republican	August 9, 1974	January 20, 1977	Completed Nixon's Second Term	Nelson A. Rockefeller
Jimmy Carter	Democrat	January 20, 1977	January 20, 1981	One	Walter Mondale
Ronald Reagan	Republican	January 20, 1981	January 20, 1989	Two	George H.W. Bush
George H.W. Bush	Republican	January 20, 1989	January 20, 1993	One	Dan Quayle
Bill Clinton	Democrat	January 20, 1993	January 20, 2001	Two	Al Gore
George W. Bush	Republican	January 20, 2001	January 20, 2009	Two	Dick Cheney
Barack Obama	Democrat	January 20, 2009			Joe Biden

"Our country abounds in the necessaries, the arts, and the comforts of life." James Madison

WRITE TO THE PRESIDENT

You may write to the president at:

**The White House
1600 Pennsylvania Avenue NW
Washington, DC 20500**

You may e-mail the president at:
comments@whitehouse.gov

GLOSSARY

amendment - a change to a country's constitution.

American Revolution - from 1775 to 1783. A war for independence between Great Britain and its North American colonies. The colonists won and created the United States of America.

Articles of Confederation - the first constitution of the United States. It was written after the Declaration of Independence, and used until March 4, 1789, when the current U.S. Constitution was ratified.

cabinet - a group of advisers chosen by the president to lead government departments.

constitution - the laws that govern a country or a state. The U.S. Constitution is the laws that govern the United States. Something relating to or following the laws of a constitution is constitutional.

debate - a contest in which two sides argue for or against something.

debt - something owed to someone, usually money.

Democratic-Republican - a member of the Democratic-Republican political party. During the early 1800s, Democratic-Republicans believed in weak national government and strong state government.

Federalist - a member of the Federalist political party. During the early 1800s, Federalists believed in a strong national government.

inaugurate (ih-NAW-gyuh-rayt) - to swear into a political office.

militia (muh-LIH-shuh) - a group of citizens trained for war or emergencies.

neutral - not taking sides in a conflict.

rebellion - an armed resistance or a defiance of a government.

rector - the leader of a school, such as a university.

revenue - the total income a nation or a state collects from sources such as taxes.

secretary of state - a member of the president's cabinet who handles relations with other countries.

Stamp Act - a law passed in 1765. It taxed all North American colonial commercial and legal papers, newspapers, pamphlets, cards, almanacs, and dice.

tutor - someone who teaches a student privately.

unconstitutional - something that goes against the laws of a constitution.

WEB SITES

To learn more about James Madison, visit ABDO Publishing Company on the World Wide Web at **www.abdopublishing.com**. Web sites about James Madison are featured on our Book Links page. These links are routinely monitored and updated to provide the most current information available.

INDEX